# Identity Journey

Developing into YOU

# Identity Journey
## Developing into YOU

*Patricia Farrenkopf, Ed.D*

*Owner and Creator of*

PGi TM
*ProGift-ify*

Fishtail Publishing

Identity Journey
© 2020 by Patricia Farrenkopf, Ed.D.

Book design by Erin O'Neil
www.erinoneil.org

Cover image by Nong Vang on Unsplash
Cover design by Erin O'Neil

Published in the USA by Fishtail Publishing LLC
Westerville, OH

www.fishtailpublishing.org

ISBN: 978-1-7333380-3-5
LCCN: 2020919218

Dedicated to all of the gifted individuals who are on their identity journey. May the experiences you have on your path show you how good being unique really is.

"We know what we are, but not what we may be."

William Shakespeare

# Table of Contents

## Acknowledgments

My dissertation committee led me to discover my own identity.

Pamela Konkol, chair
Simeon Stumme, methodologist
Paul Eisenstein, reader
the late Carol Engler, reader

# Introduction

I have been learning about, working with, and teaching teachers about gifted and high ability learners for most of my career in education. An area of interest I have always had, but did not have a name for until I was well into my teaching career, was the manner in which all children viewed themselves as learners, family members, and friends. I knew of the term "identity" but had always associated that with the '60s movement of "finding yourself." As a footnote, now that I am in my 60s, I am finding it is more important to recreate myself since I have already found myself.

My first real research into identity was through reading the work of Friedrich Nietzsche. He lived from 1844 to 1900 and believed that welcoming difficulty in life was a requirement in order to experience a fulfilling life. He believed the journey of self-discovery is one of the greatest and richest experiential challenges. In 1873, as he was approaching his thirtieth birthday, Nietzsche addressed this lifelong question of how we find ourselves and bring forth our gifts in his wonderful essay titled Schopenhauer as Educator, part of his "Untimely Meditations". In this translated resource, Nietzsche's Third Untimely Meditation is not only his salute to Schopenhauer, but also to his impression of education in a most thorough way. Many of Nietzsche's writings aimed at instructing the modern world on how to philosophize in a very rigid manner, but the hypothesis of the Third Meditation is very different and kind, specifically emphasizing that each human being is very unique. He also takes the position that true educators help us to identify the uniqueness that makes us special, but they can only point the way: "No one can build you the bridge on which you, and only you, must cross the river of life. There is one path in the world that none can walk but you. Where does it lead? Don't ask, walk!" Another quote then sent me to do further research: "There may be other methods for finding oneself, for waking up to oneself out of the anesthesia in which we are commonly enshrouded as if in a gloomy cloud — but I know of none better than that of reflecting upon one's educators and cultivators." So, I reflected on my educators and cultivators and decided more research was necessary.

Erik Homburger Erikson (1902-1995) was a German-born American developmental psychologist and psychoanalyst known for his theory on psychosocial development of human beings. He may be most famous for coining the phrase "identity crisis." Erikson never knew his own father; he was raised by his mother and stepfather, who married in 1905. He struggled with his identity throughout his youth as he felt his stepfather never fully accepted him as he did his own daughters. Erikson grew up using his stepfather's surname; he eventually adopted the name Erikson in 1939. Erikson believed that each person progressed through eight stages of development. Erikson emphasized that the environment played a major role in self-awareness, adjustment, human development, and identity. According to Erikson, youth must resolve two life "crises" during adolescence. The first crisis typically occurs during early to middle adolescence and is called the crisis of identity versus identity confusion. This crisis represents the struggle to find a balance between developing a unique, individual identity while still being accepted and "fitting in." The second crisis, occurring between late adolescence and early adulthood, is called the crisis of intimacy versus isolation. This crisis represents the struggle to resolve the reciprocal nature of intimacy; i.e., to achieve a mutual balance between giving love and support and receiving love and support.

My dissertation title, The Mirror of Erised: Exploring Identity Development in Gifted Students, is an indication that Nietzsche was not enough for me. I needed to research more.

First, I constructed my literature review. As defined by Michener, DeLamater, and Myers (2004), self-concept has been understood to be the collective thoughts we have about ourselves, including how we see our social identities and personal attributes based on our experiences.

Early on, children use role-playing to try on different personas and imagine how others would see them in that characterization. As children grow, that perspective is the collective thought of common expectations within the group of interaction. That set of expectations changes with the situation or the specific social role. It also varies depending upon the audience and the consistency of our self across those different situations and audiences.

Identities are the collective meanings assigned by each person and the others around them. Role identities are determined by the concept of self in a specific social situation. Social identity defines self in terms of the social group. Decisions regarding which identities are presented are, at times, situational. Children experience this choice when interacting in one way with academic peers in the classroom and in another way with age mates on the playground. The level of commitment to an identity is another deciding point. The network of social relationships, which are the most numerous and valued, will determine the chosen identity. We seek out friendships with those who are most like us. Need for support can be seen when an important personal thought is challenged, and either a sense of accomplishment or a simple compliment can stabilize the identity. Children have difficulty taking risks because they may be wrong and not have the support surrounding them to make the risk worthwhile.

All humans have different identities. For example, this means we can be a mother, sister, aunt, wife, employee, and student all at the same time. The hierarchy of identities is a priority list we make, either informally or thoughtfully, which orders how we define ourselves. There are events and decisions that can move those priorities to the forefront or drop them to the back. If one has spent much time and effort on identity, there is a higher investment, and the identity will be at the top of the priority list. Past praise for identity will trump those identities not receiving accolades. A sense of accomplishment for identity will translate into a high ranking of that identity. Finally, if an identity has been evaluated by a person as a defining quality, this determination will also move the identity to the front of the line.

From the research of Neihart (2009), making and keeping friends has been recognized as an important part of identity development. When considering gifted children, making and keeping friends can be more challenging than as experienced by their age mates. The gifted characteristic of asynchrony leads to gifted children seeking out friendships with older individuals who may be at their cognitive level. The gifted characteristic of advanced maturity may add the requirements of a more personal friendship and a similar viewpoint on moral and ethical issues. The need for all humans to find a place to belong may be more challenging for gifted children. As C.S. Lewis was quoted as saying, "Friendship is born at that moment when one person says to another, 'What! You too? I thought I was the only one.'"

More recent research (Kaplan & Flum, 2012) found identity formation for all populations to be a high educational priority, viewing the classrooms as "communities of learners" and the actual resulting learning as "communities of practice." Children, therefore, develop identity with certain groups and their practices. They start to identify as "historians, mathematicians, and scientists." In the school setting, these classroom placement decisions have an impact on both teaching and learning.

Sometimes these communities of learners are created through purposeful class placements. Many times, placing gifted students with others of similar ability is seen as a negative and called tracking (Fiedler, Lange, & Winebrenner, 2002). Concerns regarding the effects on general education students of homogeneously grouping gifted students have been found to be invalid. When gifted students are included in heterogeneously placed classrooms, they often are used as tutors for any students having difficulty. The gifted students often have to wait to advance their learning until everyone catches up. In addition, the gifted are usually the students who are the leaders of the classroom. There is nothing wrong with helping other students if there is an appropriate challenge provided for all students, including the gifted students. True differentiation helps all students advance at their own pace. When gifted students are grouped together, and other general education students have the opportunity to develop their capabilities, new leadership opportunities emerge for the general education students. Finally, the charge of tracking as negative has also been unfounded. If tracking causes a system of academic, social, and emotional isolation, it is a negative. If it provides a setting for students to be with others of similar interests and abilities for part of the day but also provides heterogeneous activities for the rest of the day, it is a positive.

Marcia Gross (1998) examined poetry and entries in diaries to discover the process of identity development in gifted children and adolescents. She found that identity development in gifted children and adolescents is a more complex process than it is for age peers due to the natural and nurtured differences in the two groups. If the culture in which the gifted individual is living values conformity, a mask is developed, which hides the differences and presents the acceptable behaviors. This mask hides the real passion for discovery, advanced moral sensitivities, and authentic areas of interest, which may be drastically different from age mates. If the development and wearing of this mask translates into acceptance by age mates, then they will not experience true self-acceptance and will continue to wear the mask, not wanting to reveal what is under it.

An issue connected to the decision to wear a mask or not has been bullying. According to a retrospective study (Peterson

& Ray, 2006), bullying both experienced and instigated by gifted students from K-8 has involved mostly name-calling and teasing. No significant differences were found between and among those from different sizes of cities, race/ethnographic categories, or region locations regarding either being a bully or being bullied. Peterson and Ray also found that these incidents are seldom directly reported to adults.

Gifted students, according to Silverman (2002), have experienced asynchronous development in all areas. This can translate into differences in intellectual, physical, and emotional development. Many times, gifted students are asked to act their age when, in fact, they are acting their age - or less. Cognitively, they can interact very easily with others who are older but may not socially connect with these above age individuals. Asynchrony can translate into adjustment difficulties and impact the development of identity.

For the gifted children population, Joan Freeman (2006) found that gifted children face emotional challenges but are considered to be as well-developed socially and emotionally as their non-gifted peers. Unreal expectations of those who do not understand the gifted population may cause some to think they will either have underdeveloped social skills or display natural leadership abilities. Pressure is often placed on gifted children to live up to their potential and excel in all areas, 100% of the time, although the child is gifted in just one of the many potential identification areas. Underachievement, lack of perseverance, and low attention span can be concomitant problems of the gifted. What these children need to thrive is to be with others of similar abilities, be given transparent information, time to explore their passions, and just plain be accepted as the children they are (Dai, Swanson, & Cheng, 2011).

Vialle, Heaven, and Ciarrochi (2007) examined relationships among personality factors, social support, emotional well-being, and academic achievement in a sample of 65 gifted secondary students. This sample was selected from a longitudinal study of performance data over an eight-year period of time and with a population of over 950 students. They compared these students to non-gifted peers and found that gifted students had a markedly higher academic performance for all subject areas, with the exception of geography and physical education. When teachers were asked if the gifted students were well adjusted and had fewer emotional problems than their non-gifted peers, they said that it was true. When asking the gifted students the same questions, they said they felt sadder and less satisfied with their social interactions than their non-gifted peers. Differences were not found with rankings of levels of self-esteem, trait hope, problem orientation, or attitudes toward education. When examining the gifted student population, it was found that those who earned lower grades also scored higher in psychoticism, or tough-mindedness, and lower in conscientiousness, trait hope, joviality, and attitudes towards education. It was also found that self-esteem was not related to gifted performance. Finally, there was an obvious misperception on the part of the teachers regarding how students saw their level of social adjustment and emotional challenges. This indicated that the social and emotional component of identity formation and acceptance of self should be solidly on the radar of classroom teachers and supported through educators' efforts.

By using selected literature, educators and parents can support the process and development of identity. Frank and McBee (2003) focused on a theoretical connection to *Harry Potter and the Sorcerer's Stone* (Rowling, 1997) to foster discussions with gifted adolescents about issues involving identity. The unique challenges of Harry being a gifted adolescent and realizing his giftedness was not recognized by his foster family but was at his new school resulted in selecting the main character Harry Potter as a model. This main character is certainly gifted, misunderstood, and finds his identity when being invited to attend Hogwarts School of Witchcraft. This stage of identity formation, or identity versus identity confusion (Erickson, 1968), explains Harry as well as adolescents as they find who they are now and who they want to be in future years. By analyzing adults, as Zuo and Tao (2001) found from exploring the data from Terman (1925), it was determined that achievements and emotional health later in life are greatly influenced by how identity crises are addressed in the adolescent years.

A theoretical framework serves as an interpretation of studied phenomenon. The Gifted Identity Formation Model (Mahoney, 1998) provides a "differentiated counseling model, which attempts to bridge the theoretical constructs relating to identity formation in the gifted" (p. 222). Mahoney recognizes identity formation as requiring reflection and observation to occur at the same time. He highlights this formation as it occurs through all levels of mental functioning. Mahoney also recognizes individual judgments as a result of the way others see you. Therefore, the model is a multi-dimensional context of four constructs and twelve systems that impact the identity formation of the gifted. The constructs include validation, affirmation, affiliation, and affinity.

According to Mahoney (1998), the first construct is validation, acknowledging that one's giftedness exists as corroborated by others or by oneself. Affirmation, the second construct, requires interactive acknowledgment of who we are. The third construct of affiliation is an alliance or association with others of similar intensities, passions, desires, and abilities. The fourth construct is affinity, an attraction towards that which nourishes and resembles a mating of souls, spirit, and philosophy (p. 222).

When considering systems, Mahoney described these variables that are contributors to the development of identity as a gifted individual. He pointed out that the systems do overlap, requiring an in-depth exploration of how each relates to giftedness.

The self-system has been the values and beliefs held by the gifted individual. The family system has included immediate family members. The family of origin system also has included past generations of the immediate family. The cultural system has recognized the importance of heritage, gender, race, religion, and ethnicity. The vocational system has noted career choices and development as well as occupations and vocational exposure. The environmental system has focused on the individual's living spaces at home, workspaces at school, and any surrounding included in daily life. The educational system has reviewed both the formal and informal ways the gifted child is educated. The social system has spoken to relationships with age and intellectual mates, family members, and connecting with all others in their world. The psychological system has analyzed how experiences connect with and build self-esteem and self-concept. The political system has acknowledged the political effects of decisions on how gifted education services are provided. The organic-physiological system has investigated the connection between physiological traits and being gifted. The developmental system has acknowledged the asynchronous or uneven development of the intellectual, social, and emotional behaviors of the gifted.

In conclusion, in order to "connect the dots," identity formation, as examined by Erikson (1968), has been a critical process for all humans that starts with imitation in infancy and continues through our lives. It is the key developmental process in adolescence. Self-concept leads youth to connect with their peers and impacts relationships. In trying to make sense of who they are, children and youth make comparisons to others in their environment. When this process leads to self-competence, children and youth make efforts to associate and cooperate with other children to a greater extent than if the comparison results in a less favorable likeness.

Formal operational thinking is a prerequisite for identity development (Zou and Tao, 2001). This stage begins at about age 12 and lasts into adulthood. During this time, individuals develop the ability to think about abstract concepts. Skills such as logical thought, deductive reasoning, and systematic planning also emerge during this stage.

Gifted students have entered the stages of formal

operational thinking and identity formation earlier due to their asynchronous development (Silverman, 2002). They reach the formal operational stage earlier than age peers. Silverman also examined the gifted characteristic of perfectionism and connected it to identity development. When perfectionism is an intrinsic trait, it can be a positive when it results in gifted children extending their understanding and skills. Extrinsic perfectionism is bestowed when everything the child does is received with "perfect," and they hesitate to take risks in the event they are not found to be perfect all of the time. A forced-choice dilemma (Gross, 1989) can occur when gifted students choose intimacy needs over intellectual: They wear a figurative mask to hide their intellectual interests.

The class selected for the focus of my dissertation study was one of two accelerated math classes in fifth grade. The curriculum was telescoped, meaning that both fifth and sixth grade standards were being taught during the year of this study. The gifted fifth-grade students in this study were experiencing asynchronous development, formal operational thinking, and their first telescoped accelerated math class with other students of similar ability. As they develop identity through validation, affirmation, affiliation, and affinity (Mahoney, 1998), they recognize a clear sense of challenge and preference for ownership of their learning. Friends, who were found previously to this school year, are still maintained as friends because of the similarities found in each other. The students have a growth mindset (Dweck, 2007) and they demonstrate that, through their beliefs, their abilities depend on their continual exercise and attention to learning. The students also have a high level of grit (Duckworth, 2007), not as demonstrated through taking the Grit Test, but by sharing what they do when they face a problem they do not at first know how to solve. They use strategies and keep trying until they work through the challenge to get to the next one. The grit they were born with has been reinforced with safe failure experiences and learning valuable lessons from those times (Karlgaard, 2013; Lichtman,

2014). In considering one male student's interview data, the high level of grit he indicated should be tempered with stress strategies so that his gifted characteristics and acceleration trajectory do not result in social and emotional issues down the road.

The students in this study are now in high school. I have returned to these students again, during this summer 2020 of the Global Pandemic, to ask the same qualitative research questions I asked of them asked when they were in fifth grade. I am learning more about identity development as I return to these gifted students to see where they are now on their identity journey. In addition, I have been able to connect with Andrew Mahoney, adding to the analysis of my recent interviews. This may need to be a new book for me to write.

The information and educational tools contained in this book and accompanying card decks will assist those on their own journey, whatever part of the path they are on at the moment. These resources will also assist those who are the educators and cultivators who are assisting and keeping the travelers on their path.

~ Patricia Farrenkopf ~

Before I can tell my life
what I want to do with it,
I must listen to
my life
telling me who I am.

Parker J. Palmer
Author: Let Your Life Speak
*Center for Courage and Renewal*

## The Foundation of the Journey

The foundation for the identity journey is based on the following premises...

This journey **simultaneously** involves both **reflection and observation**.

The journey **unfolds over time** and takes place **during all levels of development**.

We make **judgments along the journey** based on three lenses:

- **how we see ourselves**

- **how we perceive others see us**

- **how we interact with others who are like us**

# Shaping and Influencing the Journey
## *Four Frames*

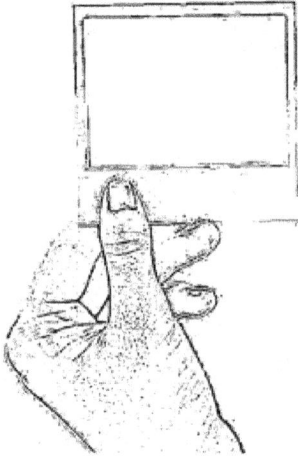

**Recognition** – The first step is the realization you are gifted.

**Confirmation** – Continued reinforcement that you are gifted.

**Connections** – Finding others who are like you.

**Preferences** – Finding the fit between your giftedness and your passion and purpose.

**First Frame**
*Recognition*

The first frame of the journey is recognizing your giftedness.

This is supported by others in your immediate community (like parents and teachers) or yourself.

These supporters are the ones you depend upon to move ahead on your journey of finding out what it means to be gifted.

This is a time when it is important to know there is support and advocacy for your giftedness.

If the definition and support is limited, then so will the development of the giftedness.

**Second Frame**
*Confirmation*

The second frame of the journey is confirmation.

This is the ongoing unfolding of what your giftedness means, supported by those same individuals who were in your immediate community when you first became aware.

This may include having enrichment added to your educational experience based on your abilities.

It might also include reinforcement by being added to a group of others participating in a gifted program option.

## Third Frame
*Connections*

The third frame of the journey involves connections.

Your own identity continues to develop as you find others who have similar sensitivities, interests, goals, and talents.

These authentic connections provide a place, both physically and mentally, where you are appreciated and accepted for being unique.

When these connections develop, you can truly be yourself and initiate and develop true friendships.

**Fourth Frame**
*Preferences*

The fourth frame is preferences.

It really blends recognition, confirmation and connections with a deepening development of your real passions, defined purposes, and friendships.

This is where you can find support from educators and contributors who know your passions and purpose and who can help you define how you can act on the goals you would like to realize.

# Compass Contributors to the Journey

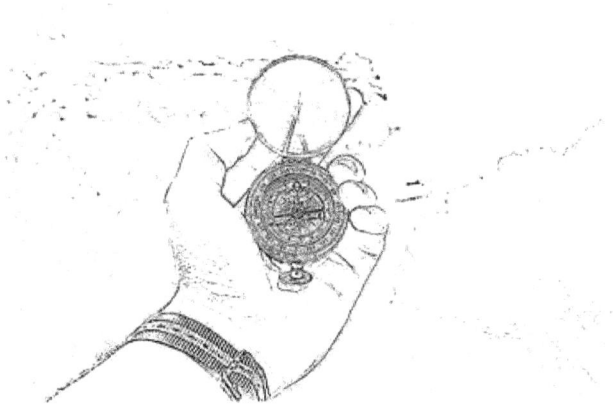

YOU
Your Immediate Family
Your Ancestry
Your Origins
Your Career Exposures
Your Living Spaces
Your Educational Routes
Your Relationships
Your Experiences
Your Legislations
Your Attributes
Your Phases

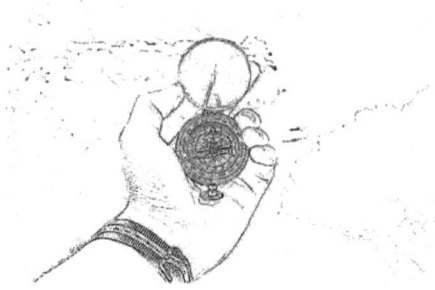

## YOU
What are YOUR values? What do you believe?
How do you see yourself as a gifted individual?
Do you think others can see what you see in yourself?

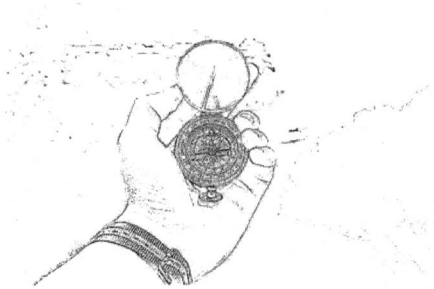

## YOUR IMMEDIATE FAMILY

How do your parents and siblings...your immediate
family members see you as a gifted individual?
How have they been able to support your journey?

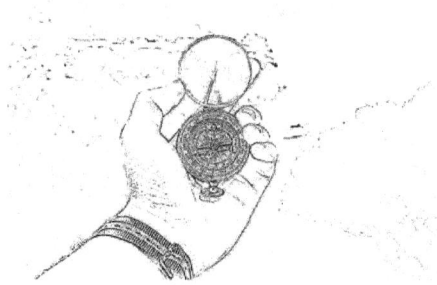

**YOUR ANCESTRY**
How well do you know the past generations
of your family?
Are their values and interests similar to yours -
or different?
What new pursuits will you be adding to
your family history?

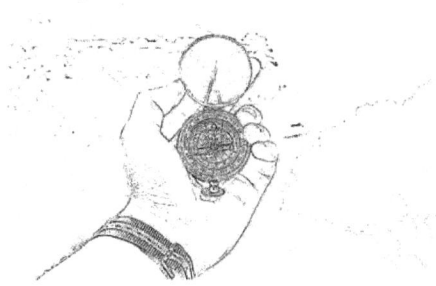

## YOUR ORIGINS
How has your heritage, gender, race, religion, and ethnicity supported your values and beliefs?
What new understandings will you be able to add to the values and beliefs typically held?

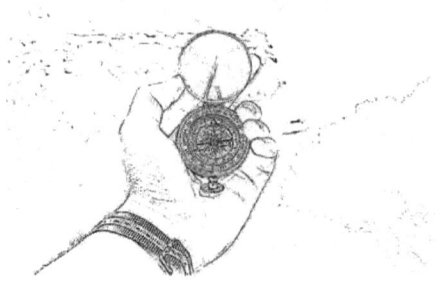

**YOUR CAREER EXPOSURES**
Which occupations or careers are you interested
in considering?
Are they the same or different from your immediate
family and even your ancestors?
What new career roles will you be adding to
your family history?

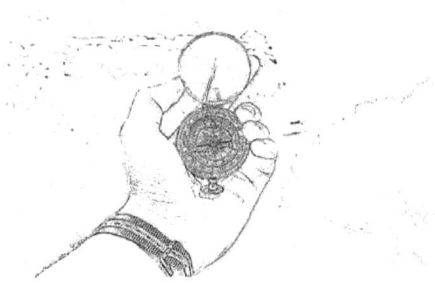

## YOUR LIVING SPACES
Where do you do your work and play in your home?
What are your work spaces like at school?
What supplies and materials do you like to have
handy when you are creating?
Is there anything you would add or change?

## YOUR EDUCATIONAL ROUTES
Where do you learn?
School may be one place, but there are other places
you can learn and other concepts to learn besides
math and science.
Are you a member of any clubs?
Do you like to do research on your own?

## YOUR RELATIONSHIPS
How do you connect with other people - and who are
the other people with whom you connect?
Do they include family members, friends, neighbors,
special interest groups and clubs?

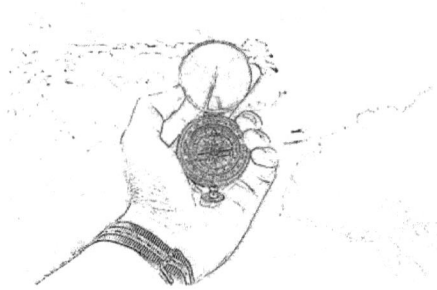

**YOUR EXPERIENCES**

Are you a person who likes to be constantly moving or
do you like to sit peacefully and read a book?
Do you like to imagine and create stories or are you
interested in factual information?
Do you like to work in a group or by yourself?

## YOUR LEGISLATIONS
Are there opportunities for you to develop
your abilities.
talents, and interests?
Where are you able to do that?
Is there a formal program available for you at your
school or do your teachers provide those opportunities
in your classroom?

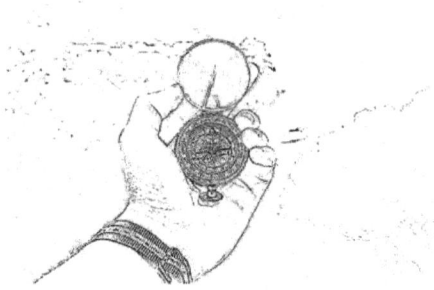

## YOUR ATTRIBUTES

Are you a math person or a reader?  Or both?
Are you a natural at problem solving or creating a
piece of art or music?
Are you a leader and like to organize people
and activities?
Are you known for your sports abilities?

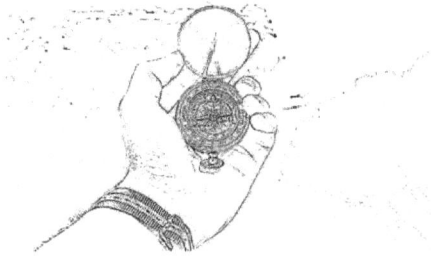

## YOUR PHASES

Which phase are you in at the moment?
Are you in elementary school or just starting
middle school?
Do you enjoy talking to individuals who are older than
you - even adults - about some topics and still like to
play with your neighborhood age mate friends?

Be who you are and say what you feel ...
because those who mind don't matter
and those who matter don't mind.

Dr. Seuss
Theodor Seuss Geisel

# Attributes
## *An Identity Journey Activity*

*Identity Circle Discussion*
You will need:
- 10 index cards per person in discussion
- Pens

*Directions*
Hand out the index cards and pens to each participant. Ask the participants to think about their attributes and what makes up their identity. Instruct them to write one attribute on each index card. They should have written down 10 values in total.

Some examples of categories that can be useful for identifying values:

| | |
|---|---|
| **family member role** | **career of interest** |
| **physical features** | **gender** |
| **occupation** | **how educated** |
| **living space** | **strongest feeling/emotion** |
| **ethnicity/culture** | **family country of origin** |
| **friends** | **activities you enjoy** |
| **beliefs** | **other ideas you have** |

*Attributes* is a "get-to-know-you" game. You will have an opportunity to discuss with many friends and family members the attributes that make up your identity and how you prioritize them in your life.

The activity works best with even numbers. Divide your group in half and make one inner circle and one outer circle. The people in the outer circle should face inside, and the people in the inner circle should face outside. Each inner circle person will pair up with an outer circle person. You can stand, sit on the floor, or use chairs.

Participants share with their first partner why they chose to write down the values they did. After sharing for 5-7 minutes, ask all participants to discard one of their cards. This part of the activity gives participants an opportunity to reflect on how they prioritize their values. After the participants discard one card, the outer circle will rotate one partner to the right. Everyone should have a new partner now. Have the new pairs discuss why they selected this card to discard.

Continue this process until all participants are each left with one card — their most important value.

**Another way to use...**

Have each person create attribute cards and order them from most important to least important.

Each person share these attributes with each other and explain each one.

This is a very easy, low-maintenance group activity that requires minimal preparation and can work for groups as small as 8 people to as large as 50 people. This activity is also good to help encourage people to share deeply with others with whom they would not otherwise share.

Be yourself;
everyone else is
already taken.

Oscar Wilde

# Guess Who?
*Modified John Rader Simulation*

On the following pages, there are descriptions of individuals. Their real names have been changed.

From the information provided, see if you can guess who these individuals are.

You might just know some of them.

**Sam Edder**
*Modified John Rader Simulation*

Age: 9 years old | Grade: 4th grade

Learning Style: Slower in math, but more thoughtful. Very creative, but can be restless and very sensitive

Makes Friends?: Likes to be alone and is very quiet

Interests: Likes to think about living in a fantasy world

Skills: Plays the violin and loves to read

Personal Goals: To be independent and be on his own

## Mary Hall
*Modified John Rader Simulation*

Age: 11 years old | Grade: 5th grade

Learning Style: Average student

Makes Friends?: Likes to be alone

Interests: Likes to daydream

Skills: Is very patient with children, older people, and those who are in hospitals

Personal Goals: Wants to help others, especially those who are poor

## Elaine Hawkins
*Modified John Rader Simulation*

Age: 12 years old | Grade: Homeschooled

Learning Style: Average learner and very creative

Makes Friends?: Likes to make people think she is older than she really is

Interests: Likes to read and go to art and history museums

Skills: Dancing

Personal Goals: To grow up and be a dancer

## Bill Ridell
*Modified John Rader Simulation*

Age: 11 years old | Grade: Homeschooled

Learning Style: Average learner, very creative

Makes Friends?: Likes to be with younger students

Interests: Mechanics and fire

Skills: Works with his hands and loves to read, but does not speak with good grammar

Personal Goals: To work hard and earn money

## Albert Wright
*Modified John Rader Simulation*

Age: 17 years old | Grade: Out of school and did not graduate

Learning Style: Very smart – self taught

Makes Friends?: Very friendly, easy going and even tempered; well-liked and respected

Interests: Physical activities, practical jokes, reading, and traveling

Skills: Self-educated by reading, good debater and arguer

Personal Goals: To be independent and be on his own

**Teddy Geisel**
*Modified John Rader Simulation*

Age: 10 years old | Grade: 5th grade

Learning Style: He is hands on and very witty. He just enters a room and, without trying, makes things funnier and happier. He surprises others – and often even himself

Makes Friends?: Is genuinely concerned for others. A treasured compatriot to a close circle of friends. Active as a Boy Scout

Interests: Animals – his dad is superintendent of the parks board and often takes Teddy to the zoo, visiting behind the scenes

Skills: His mom is his accomplice in crime by allowing him to draw animal caricatures on the plaster walls of his bedroom. She also has always sung songs to him with rhyming words. He likes to write – especially things that rhyme

Personal Goals: Wants to become a writer and an artist

**Danny Rad**
*Modified John Rader Simulation*

Age: 11 years old | Grade: 6th grade

Learning Style: all of them – visual, auditory, hands on. Very gifted and easily asks very good questions

Makes Friends?: Did not have friends at his primary school and was bullied, so he moved to a residential gifted school. He was placed in a class with two other people who became instant friends

Interests: Lives with his Aunt and Uncle who took him to the zoo. At his new school he learned a new sport and became quite good at playing it. It involved chasing a walnut-sized golden ball

Skills: Magic tricks with a jacket he got at Christmas and a mirror that was in his new school

Personal Goals: To find out more about his parents

**Emma Watts**
*Modified John Rader Simulation*

Age: 11 years old | Grade: 6th grade

Learning Style: Has a brilliant mind for academics and is gifted in almost any subject she studies. Very studious and bookish. Both of her parents are dentists who are "a bit bemused" at the uniqueness of their daughter, while also being very proud of her

Makes Friends?: At first, she may seem like a know-it-all and very unfriendly. Can step forward to pay back a favor, and becomes a true and lifelong friend

Interests: Likes to go to the library

Skills: Magic tricks and claims she can time travel

Personal Goals: To be an advocate for those who are housekeepers

**Rup Grin**
*Modified John Rader Simulation*

Age: 11 years old | Grade: 6th grade

Learning Style: Is the sixth generation of family members attending the gifted school he attends. He is a twin. Before he goes to the gifted school, he is home schooled by his mother

Makes Friends?: His two brothers are always playing pranks on him. He does make two dear friends at his gifted school. He makes sacrifices for two friends, as they do for him

Interests: playing chess (very accomplished)

Skills: He has been given a coveted award at his gifted school with extra authority and responsibilities. He also serves on a sports team with the goal of chasing a walnut-sized golden ball, guarding the three goal posts attempting to stop the other team's players from scoring

Personal Goals: He wants to reform the gifted school and eventually work in a joke shop that two of his brothers dreamed up

It is your turn to guess the real names
of these nine mystery people:

Sam Edder
Mary Hall
Elaine Hawkins
Bill Ridell
Albert Wright
Teddy Geisel
Danny Rad
Emma Watts
Rup Grin

Turn the page to check your answers...

## Sam Edder
*Albert Einstein*

Albert Einstein was born as the first child of Jewish couple Hermann and Pauline Einstein. His sister Maja Einstein observed that Albert "was never much good at the easy part of mathematics - like knowing his math facts. To shine, he had to move on to the hard part. When he became an adult, his mathematical intuition was recognized as extraordinary and he could handle deftly the most difficult of tensor calculus, but simple arithmetic calculations continued to be an area of relative weakness."

In his spare time, he liked to work on theoretical physics. He is best known for two theories - the theory of relativity and $E = mc2$. This formula states that matter can be converted into energy. **E** stands for energy, **m** for mass and **c** for the speed of the light in a vacuum.

After this theory was proven right in an experiment in 1919 (deflection of light by the sun's gravitational field), Einstein became famous overnight. In 1921, Albert Einstein won the Nobel Prize for Physics.

Albert Einstein's son Eduard once asked his father why he was so famous. Einstein said, "When a blind beetle crawls over the surface of a curved branch, it doesn't notice that the track it covered was curved. I was lucky enough to notice what the beetle didn't notice."

## Mary Hall
*Eleanor Roosevelt*

Eleanor Roosevelt was born in New York City. Although she grew up in a fairly wealthy family, she had a tough childhood. Her mother died when she was eight and her father when she was only ten. When Eleanor turned fifteen, her grandmother sent her to boarding school near London, England.

At first Eleanor was scared, however, the headmistress took a special interest her. By the time she graduated, Eleanor had gained confidence in herself. She had learned a lot about herself and life. She returned home a new person.

She married the 32nd president of the United States, Franklin D. Roosevelt, and became first lady. The job of the First Lady had always been to host parties and entertain foreign dignitaries and political leaders. Eleanor decided she could do more than this.

During World War II, she went to work for the Red Cross. She traveled to Europe and the South Pacific to visit the sick and the wounded, and to let the troops know how much they were appreciated.

For seven years she represented the United States at the United Nations (UN), which was created in large part by her husband. While a member, she helped to write the Universal Declaration of Human Rights which described that people throughout the world should be treated fairly and had certain rights that no government should be able to take away.

## Elaine Hawkins
### *Isadora Duncan*

Isadora Duncan was born in San Francisco. She was raised by her mother, Dora, a single mother and a piano teacher with a great appreciation for the arts. At the age of six, Isadora began to teach movement to little children in her neighborhood. By the time she was ten, others found out what she was doing and her classes had become really large. She requested to leave public school so that she, along with older sister Elizabeth, could earn income from teaching dance.

In the early 1900s the dancer Isadora Duncan created a new form of dance. Duncan rejected the strict rules of ballet, which was the main form of dance at the time. Duncan's free style of dancing came to be known as modern dance. She based her dancing on natural rhythms and movements.

Duncan created dance schools in the United States, Germany, and Russia, with her dance students dubbed the "Isadorables" by the media.

Duncan's autobiography, *My Life*, was published and has gone on to become a critically acclaimed work.

## Bill Ridell
*Thomas Edison*

Thomas Edison was born in Milan, Ohio and was the youngest of seven children.

Edison was often ill as a child and therefore started school later than he otherwise would have. Although he did have problems when he finally went to school, these were as a result of his social behavior and not of his mental abilities. Tom became annoyed with having to share the text with other children – he was a rapid reader and had no patience with his classmates and their pace of reading and understanding.

Tom's overworked and short-tempered teacher finally lost his patience with his persistent questioning and seemingly self-centered behavior. It was about that time that it was noticed that Tom's forehead was unusually broad and his head was considerably larger than normal, so Tom's brains were considered addled or scrambled. Tom's mom promptly withdrew Tom from school and began to "home teach" him. Not surprisingly, she was convinced her son's slightly unusual demeanor and physical appearance were merely outward signs of his remarkable intelligence. Before Tom was ten, he had read History of England, Decline and Fall of the Roman Empire, History of the World, and The Age of Reason.

Edison is considered one of the most prolific inventors of his time, holding 1,093 US patents in his name.

## Albert Wright
*Abraham Lincoln*

Abraham Lincoln was born in a single-room log cabin in Hardin County, Kentucky. His parents were Thomas and Nancy Hanks Lincoln. His father lost everything when Abraham was young and they had to move to Perry County, Indiana where they struggled to get by. When he was just nine years old, his mother died and his sister Sarah took care of him until his father remarried.

Abraham had very little formal education, but had a strong interest in books and learning. Most of what he learned was self-educated and from books he borrowed. His family later moved to Illinois where Lincoln would set out on his own.

As a young man, Lincoln worked a variety of jobs including shopkeeper, surveyor, and postmaster. For a time, he even split firewood with an axe for a living. He soon moved into politics and won a seat in the Illinois Legislature when he was 25. Lincoln served on the Illinois State Legislature for several terms. During that time, he studied the law and began to work as a lawyer. He ran for the U.S. Congress in 1845. He won the election and served as a congressman for one term. Lincoln won the 1860 election and was inaugurated as president in March of 1861. During his presidency, the Civil War started, Lincoln signed the Emancipation Proclamation, and he wrote and gave the Gettysburg Address.

## Teddy Geisel
*Dr. Seuss – Theodor Seuss Geisel*

Dr. Seuss was a beloved children's book author and illustrator. He was born on March 4, 1904 in Springfield, Massachusetts. The effect of his mother's support to draw on his bedroom walls and his father's frequent trips with him to the back streets of the zoo definitely contributed to his desire to write books about imaginary animals and with a text that rhymed. His birthday has been designated as Read Across America Day.

Dr. Seuss, first known by the name Theodore Seuss Geisel, attended Dartmouth and was the editor of the humorous publication, *Dartmough Jack-o-Lantern*. He needed to find a pseudonym to continue as the editor of this publication. That is when he thought of being called Dr. Seuss; Seuss was his mother's name before she married Mr. Geisel.

Dr. Seuss never had children of his own, so he liked to boast of the achievements of his imaginary daughter, Chrysanthemum-Pearl. He even dedicated The 500 Hats of Bartholomew Cubbins (1938) — his second children's book — to "Chrysanthemum-Pearl (aged 89 months, going on 90)."

## Danny Rad
*Daniel Radcliffe aka Harry Potter*

Harry Potter was a half-blood wizard, yet one of the most famous wizards of modern times. He was the only child born to James and Lily Potter, both respected members of the original Order of the Phoenix.

Harry was orphaned and had to be raised by his only remaining blood relative, Muggle aunt Petunia Dursley. While in her care he would be protected from Lord Voldemort, due to the Bond of Bloodcharm Albus Dumbledore placed upon him. This powerful charm would protect him until he became of age, or no longer called his aunt's house home. As the only known survivor of the Killing Curse (up to that point), Harry was already famous before he arrived at Hogwarts School of Witchcraft and Wizardry.

The Dursley family was quite cruel to Harry growing up, even forcing him to room in a broom closet and to wear their son Dudley's hand me downs. They did not treat Harry as a son as Dumbledore had hoped. They tried to discourage the use of his magic gift.

On his eleventh birthday, Harry learned that he was a wizard. He began attending Hogwarts in 1991 and was sorted into Gryffindor House with best friends Ron Weasley and Hermione Granger.

## Emma Watts
*Emma Watson aka Hermione Granger*

Hermione Granger was a Muggle-born witch born to Mr. and Mrs. Granger, both dentists. Hermione was raised as a Muggle girl until age eleven, when she learned that she was a witch and had been accepted into Hogwarts School of Witchcraft and Wizardry.

She began attending the school on September 1, 1991, where she was subsequently sorted into Gryffindor House, despite being considered for Ravenclaw. She possessed a brilliant academic mind, and proved to be a gifted student in almost every subject that she studied. She was very studious and bookish.

Hermione first met Harry Potter and Ron Weasley aboard the Hogwarts Express. Both boys found Hermione unfriendly and somewhat of an insufferable know-it-all. Later, her eagerness to please her professors and her constant correct answers reinforced their initial impression. However, in spite of the cool relationship between the three, Hermione stepped in to take the blame from Ron and Harry after they had saved her from a troll on Halloween in 1991. Harry and Ron were surprised, but grateful. The three quickly became friends.

## Rup Grin
*Rupert Grint aka Ron Weasley*

Ron Weasley was a pure-blood wizard, the sixth and youngest son of Arthur and Molly Weasley. He was also the younger brother of Bill, Charlie, Percy, Fred, George, and the elder brother of Ginny. Ron and his brothers and sister lived in the Burrow.

Ron began attending Hogwarts School of Witchcraft and Wizardry in 1991 and was sorted into Gryffindor House. He soon became best friends with fellow student Harry Potter and later Hermione Granger. Together, they faced many challenges during their adolescence, including keeping the Philosopher's Stone from Professor Quirinus Quirrell, saving Ginny from the Basilisk of the Chamber of Secrets, saving Harry's godfather Sirius Black from the Dementors of Azkaban, guiding Harry through the Triwizard Tournament, forming Dumbledore's Army and fighting in numerous battles of the Second Wizarding War: including the Battle of the Department of Mysteries (1996), Battle of the Astronomy Tower (1997), and Battle of the Seven Potters (1997). Ron also became a Gryffindor prefect and a keeper on the Gryffindor Quidditch team during his fifth year at Hogwarts. He skipped his last year of school in order to accompany Harry and Hermione on a hunt to destroy all of Lord Voldemort's Horcruxes and fought in the Battle of Hogwarts in 1998.

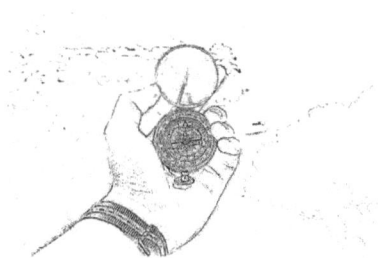

Identity Journey
Compass Contributors

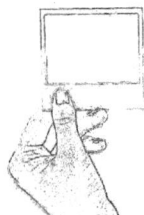

Identity Journey
Frames

**How did you do guessing the mystery people???**

Any surprises?

Did you see the Identity Journey frames and compass contributors in their descriptions?

Are there questions you now have about these people that you would like to research further?

**Some information of interest - about the Modified Identity Journey.**

Andrew Mahoney is a counselor and family therapist who developed the GIFM - Gifted Identity Formation Model. This model is from a counselor perspective so it was modified for use with children and adolescents.

When Andrew Mahoney was two years old, it was obvious to his parents that Andy had a talent in art. He remembers drawing nonstop and that his dad could not seem to buy him enough paper so he instead bought him a chalkboard.

Mahoney reflects that when he got to school he had the challenge of feeling different - he was an artist. As an adult, he rediscovered his artistic talent and passion. Go to his website to see his work: www.andymahoney.com

## Some interesting information about the Modified John Rader Simulation ... and John Rader.

John Rader was the state gifted consultant for the Indiana Department of Education in the late 1960s and 1970s. The National Defense Education Act in the late 50s led to a Title V grant focused on Identification and Encouragement of Able Students.

A group of states received this grant in the early 1970s to develop ways to identify underrepresented populations of gifted students and provide gifted professional development to teachers.

John Rader was responsible for producing the professional development materials. One tool he created was the John Rader Simulation where eight famous adults were described under pseudonyms so their identity could be revealed after the simulation.

# Who Would You Like to Research?
## *An Identity Journey Activity*

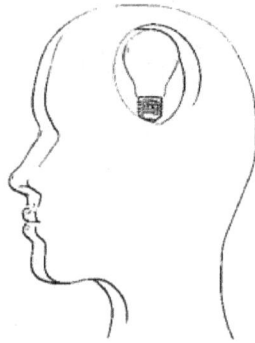

### Create Your Own "Guess Who?" Entry

Pseu·do·nym - Mystery Name:

Age:

Grade:

Learning Style:

Makes Friends?:

Interests:

Skills:

Personal Goals:

# Appendix
*Lessons from Literature*

Literature contains so many wonderful lessons from which all of us can benefit. Reading is so cherished and important for many gifted individuals. The following pages contain quotes from children's literature, beloved children's authors, and heroes/heroines teaching both gifted kids and adults important thoughts.

**Lesson:**
*Be Yourself*

"It is very frustrating not to be understood in this world. If you say one thing and keep being told that you mean something else, it can make you want to scream. But somewhere in the world there is a place for all of us, whether you are an electric form of decoration, peppermint-scented sweet, a source of timber, or a potato pancake."

— Lemony Snicket
*The Latke Who Couldn't Stop Screaming:*
*A Christmas Story*

## Lesson:
### *Celebrate being Unique and Complex*

"There's such a lot of different Annes in me. I sometimes think that is why I'm such a troublesome person. If I was just the one Anne it would be ever so much more comfortable, but then it wouldn't be half so interesting."

— L.M. Montgomery,
*Anne of Green Gables*

## Lesson:
### *You Will Find "Your Group"...You Will Be Amazed!*

"We are all a little weird and life's a little weird, and when we find someone whose weirdness is compatible with ours, we join up with them and fall in mutual weirdness and call it love."

– Dr. Seuss

"When you find people who not only tolerate your quirks but celebrate them with cries of 'Me, too!' be certain to cherish them...they are your tribe."

– A.J. Downey

## Lesson:
### *Use Your Gifts in Making Your World a Better Place*

"We can't take any credit for our talents. It's how we use them that counts."

– Madeline L'Engle,
*A Wrinkle in Time*

"It is our choices that show what we truly are, far more than our abilities."

– J.K. Rowling
*Harry Potter*

## Lesson:
### *Do Not be Afraid to Take a Risk ... and Even Fail*

"I am not afraid of storms, for I am learning how to sail my ship."

– Louisa May Alcott,
*Little Women*

"Whatever you can do, or dream you can, begin it. Boldness has genius, power and magic in it."

— Goethe

## Lesson:
### *Be in the Present*

"Yesterday is history, tomorrow is a mystery, but today is a gift. That's why we call it the present."

— A.A. Milne,
*Winnie the Pooh*

"Welcome to the present moment. Here. Now. The only moment that ever is.

— Eckhart Tolle

## Lesson:
### *Enjoy "Down" Time*

"In this modern world where activity is stressed almost to
the point of mania, quietness as a childhood need is too often
overlooked. Yet a child's need for quietness is the same today as
it has always been—it may even be greater—for quietness is an
essential part of all awareness. In quiet times and sleepy times a
child can dwell in thoughts of his own, and in songs and stories
of his own."

– Margaret Wise Brown

## Lesson:
### *When You Dream, You Can Dream BIG!*

"You are never too old to set another goal or to dream a new
dream"

– C.S. Lewis

"Listen to the mustn'ts, child,
Listen to the Don'ts
Listen to the shouldn't
The Impossible, the won'ts
Listen to the never haves
Then listen close to me –
Anything can happen child,
Anything can be."

– Shel Silverstein

PAT FARRENKOPF, ED.D

"How do we know imagination isn't just a different way of knowing something? A message from outside."

— Stephanie S. Tolan
*Welcome to the Ark*

## Lesson:
### *Pay Attention to What Your Heart is Telling You*

"Eyes are blind. You have to look with the heart!"

– Antoine de Saint-Exupéry
*The Little Prince*

"The only thing worse than being blind is having sight but no vision."
– Helen Keller

## Lesson:
### *Have Confidence in Yourself*

"Promise me you'll always remember: You're braver than you believe, and stronger than you seem, and smarter than you think."

– A. A. Milne,
*Winnie the Pooh*

"The person who follows the crowd will usually go no further than the crowd. The person who walks alone is likely to find himself in places no one has ever seen before."

– Albert Einstein

**What other books and quotes
would YOU suggest to add to this list?**

# Reference List

Dai, D.Y., Swanson, J.A. & Cheng, H. (2011). State of research on giftedness and gifted education: A survey of empirical studies published during 1998-2010. *Gifted Child Quarterly*, 55(2), 126-138.

Farrenkopf, P. (2014). Dissertation: *The mirror of erised: Exploring identity development in gifted students.* Concordia University of Chicago: River Forest, IL.

Fiedler, Ellen D. & Lange, Richard E. & Winebrenner, Susan (2002). In search of reality: Unraveling the myths about tracking, ability grouping, and the gifted. *Roeper Review*, 24(3), 108-111.

Frank, A. and McBee, M. (2003). The use of Harry Potter and the sorcerer's stone to discuss identity development with gifted adolescents. *Journal of Secondary Gifted Education*, 15(10), 33-38.

Freeman, J. (2006). The emotional development of gifted and talented children. *Gifted and Talented International*, 21(2), 20-28.

Gross, M.U.M. (1998). The me behind the mask: Intellectually gifted students and the search for identity. *Roeper Review*, 20(3), 167-173.

Kaplan, A. & Flum, H. (2013). Identity formation in educational settings: A critical focus for education in the 21st century. *Contemporary Educational Psychology*, 37, 171-175.

Lewis, C.S. (n.d.). Quotation Details. Retrieved from:www.quotationspage.com/quote/25736.html

Mahoney, A.S. (1998). In search of the gifted identity: From abstract concept to workable counseling constructs. *Roeper Review*, 20(3), 222-226.

Michener, H. Andrew, John D. DeLamater, and Daniel J. Myers (2004). *Social psychology*. 5th ed. Belmont, CA: Wadsworth/Thompson Learning.

Neihard, M. (2009). Finding true peers. *Duke TIP.* Retrieved from: www.tip.duke.edu/node/914

Nietzsche F., author; Daniel Breazeale, D., editor; Hollingdale, R. J., translator (1996). *Nietzsche: Untimely Meditations.* New York, NY: Cambridge University Press.

Nietzsche, F., author and Pellerin, D., translator (2014). *Schopenhauer as Educator: Nietzsche's Third Untimely Meditation.* Colorado Springs, CO: CreateSpace Independent Publishing Platform.

Peterson, J. & Ray, K (2006). Bullying and the gifted: Victims, perpetrators, prevalence, and effects. *Gifted Child Quarterly,* 50(2), 148-168.

**References for GIFM and Rader Simulation**

Jolly, J. (2009). The National Defense Education Act.

*Gifted Child Today* 32(2). Retrieved from: https://files.eric.ed.gov/fulltext/EJ835843.pdf

Mahoney, A. (2015). *Counseling the Gifted - Finding Self.* Retrieved from: www.counselingthegifted.com

Zirkel, P. (2005). The Law on Gifted Education. NRCGT

*Scholar Series.* Retrieved from: https://nrcgt.uconn.edu/wp-content/uploads/sites/ 953/2015/04/rm05178R.pdf

# Developing the Gifted Series
## Order at www.fishtailpublishing.org

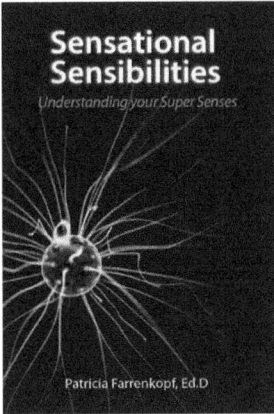

**Volume 1**
Sensational Sensibilities
*Card deck available for purchase*

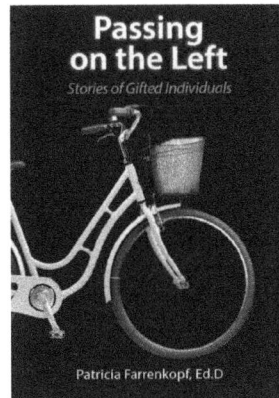

**Volume 2**
Identity Journey
*Card deck and activity sheet
available for purchase*

**Volume 3**
Myth or Reality?
*Card deck available for purchase*

**Volume 4**
Passing on the Left
*Card deck and activity sheet
available for purchase*

Fishtail Publishing

www.ingramcontent.com/pod-product-compliance
Lightning Source LLC
Chambersburg PA
CBHW021201090426
42740CB00008B/1189